ANYTIME RESET

Break the Burnout Chain

Lorrie Penn Hunter

Published by Carter & Penn LLC, Ashburn, VA.

This book is provided for informational and educational purposes only. It is not intended as, and should not be construed as, professional, legal, medical, financial, or psychological advice. The reader is responsible for their own decisions and actions.

The views expressed in this book are those of the author and do not necessarily reflect the views of any organization or entity with which the author may be affiliated.

ISBN: 978-1-7359734-6-3

Printed in the United States of America.

www.carterpenn.com / IG @carterandpenn

Acknowledgments

This book was born out of repeated cycles, real-life circumstances, and real lessons learned along the way. I was navigating yet another season of burnout and recognized that I had been here before and would conquer it yet again.

To my family — thank you for your patience and steadiness through long seasons of building and rebuilding. I tend to work quietly and carry more than I should, but your encouragement and support mean more than I can put into words.

To my friends — fellow entrepreneurs and business owners— your resilience, honesty, and drive helped shape the clarity behind these pages. Instead of resting, I wanted to build something that might help others — while I was working through it myself. Doing the most as usual.

My hope is that this book, along with my *Reset… Then Rise Again Workshop*, can help every person who has quietly carried too much. Let this be a reminder to adjust and reset your balance before burnout can take hold of you again.

The moment you realize you're burned out is often the moment you have the least capacity to fix it.

This book exists to meet you there—and help you reset before pushing through makes things worse.

Foreword

I didn't set out to write a book about burnout.

I wrote this because I reached a point where I knew something was wrong—and I couldn't find anything that actually helped. Not because there weren't books about burnout, but because most of what I found didn't match where I was.

I wasn't falling apart.
I wasn't unmotivated.
I was still functioning.

But I was tired in a way that rest didn't fix.
Anxious in ways I couldn't explain.
And far enough into burnout that I didn't know where to start climbing out.

Most advice assumed I needed more discipline, a better plan, or a dramatic reset. What I needed was something simpler and steadier—something that acknowledged how capable people experience burnout, and how hard it can be to regain clarity once you're already there.

That's why this book exists.

Not to fix you.
Not to push you.
Not to tell you to start over.

But to help you notice what's happening sooner, understand why it repeats, and learn how to Reset in a way that doesn't make things worse.

You don't need to read this quickly.
You don't need to follow it perfectly.

You only need to take what helps—and leave the rest.

That's enough.

Table of Contents

1

Burnout doesn't look the same for everyone—***but it almost always begins when life quietly exceeds capacity.***

This book isn't here to diagnose you or tell you what you should have done differently.

It's here to help you recognize what burnout actually looks like when you're still functioning—and to offer a steadier way forward.

You won't be asked to overhaul your life or push yourself harder. We'll start by noticing what's happening, without judgment, and build from there.

When the Lights Finally Come On

Burnout doesn't usually start with collapse.

It starts with a quiet realization:
Something isn't right—and I don't know how to fix it.

By the time that thought shows up, burnout is often already well underway.

You're still functioning.
Still handling responsibilities.
Still getting things done—just not the way you used to.

And that's confusing.

The Moment You Start to Notice

For many people, awareness doesn't come during the busiest stretch.

It comes *after*—when you finally slow down enough to notice how far gone you feel.

It might look like this:

You sit down to start something important.
You open your laptop.
Then you check your phone "for a minute."

An hour later, you're still scrolling.

Nothing restorative.
Nothing intentional.

Just avoidance.

You close the app, tell yourself you'll start fresh tomorrow, and feel a mix of guilt and relief.

That's not laziness.
That's burnout showing itself.

When Procrastination Isn't About Time Management

At full burnout, procrastination doesn't look like disorganization.

It can show up in subtle but familiar ways:

- avoiding things you normally handle easily
- delaying decisions because everything feels heavier than it should
- pushing tasks until "tomorrow" again and again
- restarting days instead of finishing them

You may even make plans to catch up—lists, schedules, fresh starts—but never feel less overwhelmed.

The issue isn't planning.

It's capacity.

Other Signs You Might Recognize

When burnout has fully arrived, it often shows up in everyday moments:

- snapping at people you care about over small things
- feeling irritated by questions or interruptions
- withdrawing socially—not because you don't care, but because you don't have the energy

- choosing isolation because explaining how you feel feels like too much

You might think:
Why am I reacting like this?
This isn't who I am.

You're right.

It's not who you are.
It's what happens when you've been operating past your limits for too long.

Why This Is Especially Hard for Capable People

When burnout hits, the instinct is often to look for a better system, a stronger plan, or a cleaner structure. That response makes sense—you're used to solving problems. But planning doesn't help if the problem isn't organization. And pushing doesn't help if the problem isn't effort.

Why Help Is Hard to Find at This Point

Most advice at this stage feels wrong. It assumes you have the energy to overhaul things, that you need more motivation, or that you haven't tried hard enough. What's often missing is something practical that meets you where you actually are—still showing up, aware something is wrong, unsure where to start, and unwilling to burn yourself out even more trying to recover. This book starts here on purpose.

This Is Not a Book About Fixing You

If you're here, you don't need to be told to try harder. You've already been doing that. What you need is a way to recognize what's happening, steady yourself, regain clarity, and take the next step without adding more pressure.

I've seen how often capable people miss these signs—not because they aren't paying attention, but because they're still managing.

2

Burnout repeats not because you didn't recover, ***but because the early signs weren't recognized in time.***

The Burnout Cycle

Once you recognize burnout, another realization often follows:

This isn't the first time I've felt this way.

Burnout tends to repeat—not because you're doing something wrong, but because the pattern is easy to miss while you're in it.

How the Cycle Starts (Again)

For many people, burnout doesn't start with stress.

It starts with **pressure that makes sense**.

A busy season at work.
A family obligation.
A personal goal you care about.

You tell yourself:
This is temporary. I can handle it.

And for a while, you do.

When Pushing Becomes the Default

As pressure increases, pushing becomes automatic.

You:

- stay up later to finish things
- skip breaks to keep moving

- respond quickly to avoid falling behind
- tell yourself you'll rest once things calm down

From the outside, you look productive.

From the inside, something starts to tighten.

The Shift You Don't Catch Right Away

You might notice yourself scrolling instead of starting, rereading the same message without responding, or avoiding decisions because they feel heavier than they should. You tell yourself tomorrow will be different.

You explain it away.
I'm just tired.
It's been a long week.
I'll reset tomorrow.

Tomorrow becomes next week.

When Anxiety and Guilt Enter the Picture

As burnout deepens, anxiety often follows. You start worrying about falling behind, letting people down, losing momentum, or not being as capable as you used to be. At the same time, guilt shows up.

You know what needs to be done—but you don't have the energy to do it.

So you push again.

That's how the cycle tightens.

The Forced Pause

Eventually, something forces a pause.

It might show up as exhaustion that rest doesn't fix, a short temper you don't recognize, pulling away from people because you don't have anything left, or feeling emotionally flat or overwhelmed.

You slow down—not by choice, but by necessity.

Only then does the awareness fully land:
I'm burned out.

Why Rest Alone Doesn't Break the Cycle

At this point, many people rest just enough to function again.

A weekend.
A few lighter days.
A brief break.

Energy returns—but only temporarily.

Nothing about the cycle itself changes—only your ability to tolerate it.

So when pressure ramps up again, the pattern repeats itself.

The Burnout Chain

Here's what's actually happening:

Pressure leads to pushing.
Pushing leads to depletion.
Depletion leads to anxiety or avoidance.
Avoidance leads to guilt.
Guilt leads back to pushing.

That's the burnout chain.

Breaking it doesn't require eliminating stress.

It requires interrupting the cycle **earlier**—before exhaustion and guilt take over.

Change the Pattern

Don't wait for the forced pause. Notice burnout sooner, respond earlier, and adjust your pace before capacity is gone. Burnout doesn't lose power because you avoid it—it loses power because you recognize the pattern in time.

3

Recognizing you're burned out doesn't always make the next step clear.

Why It's So Hard to Know Where to Start

One of the most frustrating moments in burnout is this:

You finally realize what's wrong—
and still have no idea what to do next.

You know you're burned out.
You know something must change.

But everything feels too tangled to touch.

Awareness Doesn't Bring Immediate Clarity

Awareness often arrives after your energy is already depleted, confidence is shaky, and decisions feel heavier than they should. So instead of relief, you feel stuck.

You might think, I see the problem… so why can't I fix it?

That question alone can make burnout feel worse.

Burnout Shrinks Your Decision-Making Ability

Burnout doesn't just make you tired.

It changes how your brain processes choices.

When you're burned out:

- everything feels urgent
- nothing feels clearly important
- even small decisions require more effort

You're not losing intelligence.

You're experiencing reduced mental flexibility.

Your system is trying to conserve energy by narrowing options.

Why "Just Make a Plan" Falls Flat

At this stage, well-meaning advice often misses the mark. You're told to reorganize, reprioritize, create a new system, or get disciplined again.

But planning assumes you have mental bandwidth, emotional steadiness, and spare energy. When you're burned out, you just don't!

So planning doesn't feel helpful—it feels like pressure. And pressure increases paralysis.

The Self-Criticism That Makes Things Harder

When clarity doesn't return quickly, self-judgment often takes over. You might find yourself thinking-- *Why can't I just get it together? I've handled worse than this. Other people don't seem this stuck.*

That internal pressure doesn't motivate recovery. It drains energy further.

Burnout isn't a character flaw. It's a capacity issue.

Why You Feel Pulled to Do Everything—or Nothing

Burnout often creates two opposing urges:

- fix everything at once, or
- avoid everything entirely

Trying to fix everything requires energy you don't have.
Avoiding everything increases guilt and anxiety.

That back-and-forth is exhausting—and common.

It's also a sign that pausing and recalibrating needs to come before solutions.

Reset Comes Before Direction

When burnout is at its height, the goal isn't progress.

It's orientation.

Before you decide:

- what to change
- what to keep
- what to let go

You need enough steadiness to think clearly again.

That's why this book doesn't start with action steps.

It starts with:

- awareness
- relief
- pacing

Direction comes later.

You've Been Here Before (Even If You Didn't Call It Burnout)

Before you move on, pause for a moment.

This probably isn't the first time you've felt overwhelmed, exhausted, or stretched beyond your limits.

Think back.

There was likely another season when:

- things felt unsustainable
- you weren't sure how you'd get through
- you had to slow down, adjust, or change course

And yet—you did.

You may not have called it burnout.
You may not have had a framework.

But you adapted.

You rested.
You recalibrated.
You found your footing again.

That matters.

Burnout doesn't erase your ability to recover.
It temporarily obscures your confidence in it.

This Time, You're Doing It With Awareness

What's different now isn't that you're struggling.

It's that you're noticing sooner—and choosing to respond intentionally.

You don't need to prove you can push through again.

You need a way to Reset *before* pushing becomes the only option.

That's what comes next.

4

A pause is often the most productive place to start when everything feels off.

Pause Before You Push

When something feels off, the instinct is often to push harder:

to catch up,
to reorganize, and
to power through until things feel normal again.

That instinct makes sense.

But it's also what keeps burnout going.

Why Pausing Feels So Uncomfortable

You might worry that if you slow down, you'll fall behind, things will pile up, or momentum will disappear. So instead of pausing, you tighten your grip. You push through discomfort, ignore early signals, and tell yourself you'll rest later.

A Pause Is Not the Same as Stopping

Pausing doesn't mean quitting.

It doesn't mean giving up on what matters.

It means creating just enough space to regain your footing.

A pause can be:

- stepping back before responding

- delaying a decision until clarity returns
- taking a short break instead of pushing through fatigue
- choosing not to add one more thing to an already full day

These pauses are small—but they're powerful.

They interrupt the burnout chain.

The Cost of Skipping a Pause

Without making space for a pause, the pressure that's been building toward burnout begins to compound.

Tasks feel heavier.
Decisions feel harder.
Your tolerance drops.

You may notice:

- impatience showing up faster
- mistakes creeping in
- frustration spilling into places it doesn't belong

These aren't signs you're failing.

They're signs you've been pushing without a pause for too long.

The Purpose of a Pause

This moment isn't asking for action.
It's asking for space.

Think of it like a yield sign. You're not stopping completely—you're slowing just enough to see clearly before moving forward.

Before you change direction, you need to:

- settle your nervous system
- reduce internal pressure
- create room to think clearly again

Pause creates that room.

Try This Now

Take a moment and ask yourself:

- Where am I pushing simply because I don't know what else to do?
- What would happen if I paused *before* reacting here?
- What's one thing I could delay or soften today without consequence?

You're not deciding what comes next yet.

You're just giving yourself space.

This Is Where Your Reset Begins

Resetting doesn't start with action.
It starts with restraint.

With choosing not to push just because you can.

Pausing here doesn't slow you down.

It prevents you from burning out again while trying to recover.

5

You don't rebuild momentum by doing everything—**you rebuild it one step at a time.**

Start Small to Regain Momentum

After a pause, the next instinct is often to do *everything*.

To make up for lost time.
To fix what feels behind.
To regain control all at once.

That urge is understandable.

It's also where momentum often slips away instead of building.

Why Big Fixes Backfire

When you're depleted, big plans feel overwhelming—even if they're good ones.

You might:

- create a long list and avoid it
- outline a plan and never start
- feel motivated briefly, then crash

This isn't a motivation problem.

It's a mismatch between effort and capacity.

Momentum doesn't come from doing more.

It comes from doing **something manageable**—and finishing it.

Small Wins Rebuild Confidence

When burnout is present, confidence is often the first thing to go—not because you're incapable, but because everything takes more effort than it used to. Tasks feel heavier. Progress feels slower. And even when you try, it can feel like nothing sticks.

Small wins change that. They restore a sense of capability, reduce mental resistance, and create forward motion without pressure.

A small win reminds you: *I can still move.*

What "Small" Actually Means

Small doesn't mean insignificant.

It means realistic.

A small step is one that:

- fits your current energy
- doesn't require perfect focus
- can be completed without pushing

Examples might include:

- responding to one priority message instead of clearing your inbox
- outlining the next step of a task instead of finishing them all

- organizing one drawer, folder, or surface
- choosing one priority for the day and letting the rest wait

Small is not a downgrade.

It's a strategy.

Completion Builds Energy

One of the fastest ways to regain momentum is to finish something. Completion builds energy.

Before adding more, finish one thing. Acknowledge it. Let the win land.

You don't need to reward yourself or move the goalposts. You just need to notice that progress happened. That recognition matters.

Try This Now

Choose one thing you've been avoiding.

Ask yourself:

- What's the smallest version of this I could complete today?
- What would "done enough" look like?

Then stop there.

Not because you can't do more—but because you don't need to.

Momentum Grows from Here

Once momentum returns, clarity often follows.

Not all at once.
Not dramatically.

But steadily.

Starting small creates space for energy to return. It lets you move forward at a pace that feels manageable, rebuilds confidence through completion, and helps momentum take shape again—naturally, without force.

6

The most effective Reset is the one that works with how you're wired—**not against it.**

Find What Works for You

By this point, you may already feel a small shift. Not a full recovery. Not everything solved. But steadier.

You've created space to pause. You've taken a few small steps. And that matters—because it's often enough to remind you that something *is* changing.

That steadiness is what allows you to start trusting yourself again.

There Is No Single Right Way to Reset

One of the fastest ways to derail progress is to assume there's a universal solution.

What works for one person may drain another.

Some people regain energy through structure.
Others need flexibility.

Some reset by organizing.
Others reset by stepping away.

None of these approaches are wrong.

The mistake is trying to force yourself into a method that doesn't fit.

Why Copying Someone Else's System Fails

When you're burned out, it's tempting to borrow solutions. You see what works for others and think, *If I just did that, I'd feel better.*

But borrowed systems often fail because they don't match how you process information, how you recover energy, or how you respond to pressure. What restores one person can overwhelm another.

A reset only works when it aligns with how you actually operate.

Pay Attention to Your Patterns

You don't need a quiz or a label to start noticing patterns.

Think about the times when you felt more balanced.

Ask yourself:

- When do I feel most focused?
- What drains me faster than it should?
- What kinds of tasks energize me—even a little?
- What kinds of tasks create resistance immediately?

These questions aren't about judgment or diagnosis. They're simply a way to start noticing what works for you.

Energy Is Information

How you feel after doing something matters more than how productive it looks.

Pay attention to:

- tasks that leave you clearer instead of depleted
- activities that restore energy rather than consume it
- rhythms that support consistency instead of forcing bursts

Your energy isn't something you're meant to push through endlessly. It's something you learn to respond to—and restore.

Try This Now

Think about one recent day.

Ask yourself:

- What gave me energy—even slightly?
- What drained me more than expected?

Don't fix anything yet.

Just notice.

Awareness is the first step toward choosing better on purpose.

Self-Trust Is a Part of Your Reset

Burnout often erodes trust in yourself.

You stop believing your instincts.
You second-guess your pace.
You override your signals.

A reset can restore that trust.

Not by forcing confidence—but by listening to yourself and responding differently.

Finding what works for you isn't indulgent. It's necessary.

The more you pay attention to what works for you, the easier it becomes to reset your pace with confidence.

7

Balance isn't about doing all the things—**it's about allocating your energy as life shifts.**

Balance Shifts as Life Shifts

When people hear the word *balance*, they often picture everything being evenly distributed.

Equal time.
Equal energy.
Equal attention.

That version of balance isn't realistic—and it's not helpful.

Why "Doing It All" Creates More Pressure

When you try to balance everything at once, it usually leads to one of two outcomes:

- you stretch yourself too thin, or
- you feel like you're constantly failing

Life doesn't operate in equal parts.

Different seasons require different allocations of time, focus, and energy.

Balance isn't about keeping everything even.

It's about choosing what gets more—*for now.*

Balance Is About Allocation

Think of balance as a **reallocation of your existing resources**.

- time
- focus
- energy
- rest

You already have these resources—you're just deciding how to use them.

Balance asks:

- Where is most of this going right now?
- Where does it need to go instead?

Sometimes a personal goal needs more attention. Sometimes family or health becomes the priority. Sometimes work requires a heavier lift.

That doesn't mean everything else disappears.

It means it gets **less for the moment**.

What Reallocation Looks Like in Real Life

Balance might look like:

- giving 60% of your energy to one priority while others run at 20%

- intentionally lowering expectations in one area to protect another
- choosing progress in one container instead of pressure in all of them

This isn't neglect.

It's strategy.

Trying to give everything 100% is often what creates burnout in the first place.

Why This Approach Feels More Sustainable

When you reallocate instead of forcing balance:

- pressure decreases
- clarity improves
- decision-making gets easier

You stop asking:
How do I balance everything?

And start asking:
What deserves more of me right now?

That shift changes everything.

Try This Now

Think about the next few weeks.

Ask yourself:

• What's on my plate right now?
• Where does my focus need to go most?
• What can temporarily receive less of my capacity — without real consequence?
• When might I need to shift again?

Write down one intentional reallocation you can make.

No overhaul required.

Just a conscious choice.

Balance Moves as Life Moves

Balance isn't something you achieve once.

It's something you adjust as life changes.

When you treat balance as flexible instead of fixed, it becomes supportive instead of stressful.

It starts working *with* your life instead of against it.

8

You can only do so much — **ignoring that reality is how burnout takes hold.**

Work Within Your Capacity

One of the most overlooked parts of burnout is this:

You don't stop because you're incapable.
You stop because you've exceeded your capacity.

That distinction matters.

What Capacity Actually Means

Capacity isn't about how much you *should* be able to handle.

It's about how much you can realistically support **right now**—with the energy, focus, and emotional bandwidth you currently have.

Capacity shifts.

It changes with:

- stress levels
- life circumstances
- health
- emotional load

Ignoring capacity doesn't make it go away.

It just makes burnout arrive faster.

Capacity isn't fixed—and it isn't a verdict. It's simply information you can work with to find your current balance.

Why We Keep Operating Past It

Many capable people are used to stretching themselves.

You've handled more before.
You've pushed through harder seasons.
You've made it work when things felt impossible.

So when capacity shrinks, the instinct is to override it.

You tell yourself:

- *I'll catch up soon.*
- *This is just temporary.*
- *I can handle this like I always do.*

Sometimes that's true.

Often, it's how burnout repeats.

How Capacity Signals Show Up

When you're operating past capacity, effort starts to feel different. Not dramatic—just heavier than it should. You might notice:

- tasks taking longer than usual
- simple decisions feeling draining
- increased anxiety or self-doubt
- a sense of pressure without clear urgency

These aren't warning signs that something is wrong with you. They're signals that you're asking more of yourself than your current capacity can support.

You're still functioning—but at a cost.

That cost accumulates quietly.

Capacity Is Not a Personal Failing

Working within capacity doesn't mean lowering standards forever.

It means adjusting expectations **temporarily,** so you don't deplete yourself completely.

Athletes train within limits to avoid injury. Businesses adjust operations during high-demand periods.

People recover by pacing—not pushing. Burnout recovery follows the same logic.

Try This Now

Ask yourself:

- What am I asking of myself right now that exceeds my current capacity?
- When does "a lot" turn into *too much* for me?
- What would it look like to scale that back—just slightly?

This isn't about doing less everywhere.

It's about choosing where effort makes sense today.

Capacity-Based Progress Builds Stability

When you work within capacity, things start to feel steadier.

- anxiety decreases
- confidence stabilizes
- consistency becomes possible again

Progress doesn't disappear when you honor capacity. It becomes more sustainable.

You're not slowing down.

You're protecting your ability to keep going—steadily and sustainably.

9

Stability must come before pace if you want progress to last.

Slow Down to Restore Stability

Once you begin to feel a little better, a familiar urge often returns:

I need to move faster now.

To catch up.
To make up for lost time.
To prove you're back.

That urge is understandable.

It's also where many people unintentionally restart the burnout cycle.

Why Speed Feels Necessary

Speed often feels like safety.

Moving quickly can feel like:

- regaining control
- reducing anxiety
- preventing things from slipping

But speed doesn't actually create stability.

It masks instability—temporarily.

When burnout is still present, pushing for speed often reintroduces pressure before your system is ready.

What Stability Actually Looks Like

Stability isn't about doing more.

It's about feeling steady while doing what you're already doing.

Signs of growing stability include:

- less mental resistance when starting tasks
- fewer spikes of anxiety
- clearer thinking
- the ability to stop without guilt

These are subtle shifts, but they're signs that your system is settling.

They indicate that Reset is taking hold.

Why Rushing Undermines Recovery

When you rush:

- mistakes increase
- tolerance drops
- pressure returns quickly

You may not notice it immediately.

But your system does.

And it responds by tightening again—through fatigue, avoidance, or anxiety.

Restoring stability first prevents this rebound.

Pace Creates Confidence

Confidence doesn't come from speed. It comes from consistency. When you move at a pace you can maintain, trust in yourself starts to return. Anxiety softens. Momentum becomes reliable instead of fragile.

That kind of confidence lasts because it's built on stability—not pressure.

Try This Now

Ask yourself:

- Where am I trying to speed up too soon?
- What would happen if I stayed at this pace a little longer?

Slowing here isn't a setback.

It's reinforcement.

Speed Will Come—When It's Supported

When stability is present, speed doesn't feel forced. It doesn't feel like catching up or proving something. It feels steady. Intentional. Sustainable.

You won't have to convince yourself you're ready.
You'll notice that tasks feel lighter.
Decisions feel clearer.
Momentum returns without strain.

That's the difference between pushing and progressing.

Stability creates the foundation that pace can build on. When you honor that order — steady first, then faster — you stop repeating the burnout cycle.

You don't have to rush to move forward.
You just have to move from a place that can support you.

10

It's much easier to interrupt burnout when you catch it early—**before the pattern gains momentum.**

How to Notice Burnout on Its Approach

Burnout rarely arrives without warning.

The signals are there long before exhaustion forces you to stop.

The challenge is noticing them *while you're still moving.*

Burnout Approaches Quietly

Early burnout doesn't always feel dramatic.

It often shows up as subtle internal shifts:

- increased worry about things you normally handle
- second-guessing decisions you once made easily
- feeling tense without a clear reason
- carrying a low-level sense of pressure throughout the day

Nothing looks "wrong" on the surface.

But inside, something is tightening.

When Anxiety Is the First Signal

For many people, anxiety—not exhaustion—is the first sign of burnout's approach.

You might notice:

- racing thoughts about falling behind
- imagining negative outcomes before they happen
- worrying about your performance or reliability
- questioning your ability to keep up

Confidence begins to wobble.

Not because you've changed—but because your system is overloaded.

Panic Is Often About Capacity, Not Danger

As burnout progresses, anxiety can tip into panic.

Not full panic attacks—but moments where:

- everything feels urgent at once
- your chest feels tight
- your thoughts jump ahead faster than you can manage

This isn't a sign that something is wrong with you.

It's a sign that your capacity is being exceeded.

Your nervous system is asking for relief.

The Early Signals Are Easy to Dismiss

Because these signals don't look dramatic, they're easy to rationalize:

- *I'm just stressed.*
- *This will pass once things calm down.*
- *Everyone feels like this sometimes.*

And sometimes, they do pass.

But when they repeat, they're information.

Ignoring them doesn't make them go away.

It just delays response.

Why Early Awareness Changes Everything

Noticing burnout early gives you options.

You can:

- pause before anxiety escalates
- adjust pace before pressure compounds
- reallocate energy before exhaustion sets in

Early response doesn't require drastic change.

It requires attention.

Try This Now

Over the next few days, pay attention to moments when something feels slightly off—not overwhelming, just different.

Notice:
- when worry shows up faster than usual
- when confidence dips without a clear reason
- when urgency feels emotional instead of practical

When you notice one of these signals, don't push past it. Pause and ask yourself: *What would help me feel steadier right now?*

That might mean slowing your pace, postponing a decision, or reallocating your energy for the day. You're not fixing anything yet—you're interrupting the pattern early.

This Is Where Prevention Begins

Burnout loses its grip when it's recognized early.

Noticing the signals sooner gives you choices—before pressure builds, before anxiety escalates, before exhaustion takes over.

You don't have to wait for collapse. You don't have to push until you can't.

Early awareness allows you to respond while you still have room to adjust.

That's how burnout stops gaining ground—and how prevention actually works.

11

The faster you respond to burnout signals, **the less power burnout has over you.**

Shorten the Distance Between the Signals and Your Reset

Noticing burnout is important.
Responding to it sooner is what changes the outcome.

The longer the gap between the signal and the response, the more pressure builds—and the harder a reset becomes. Burnout doesn't usually escalate all at once. It gains momentum in the space between *noticing something feels off* and *doing something about it.*

Shortening that distance is one of the most effective ways to reduce burnout's impact.

Why We Wait Too Long to Respond

Most people don't ignore burnout signals on purpose. They delay because the early signs feel manageable. Pausing feels inconvenient. Responding feels like overreacting.

So instead of adjusting, you push a little longer. Then a little longer after that.

You tell yourself you'll deal with it after this meeting, this deadline, this week. And by the time you circle back, the pressure has already compounded. The distance between the signal and your response quietly grows.

When Panic Triggers the Wrong Response

When signals are ignored long enough, responses often come from panic instead of awareness.

You might suddenly feel the urge to reorganize everything, create a new plan, set aggressive deadlines, or overhaul routines all at once. These actions can look productive—but they often happen while you're still in a state of instability, before a pause, before clarity has returned.

A new plan created from panic doesn't address burnout. It often adds pressure on top of it. The structure changes, but the behaviors—and the pace—stay the same.

A Reset Works Best When It's Small and Timely

A reset doesn't need to be dramatic to be effective. In fact, the most powerful resets usually happen earlier and look quieter than you expect.

They can happen when you pause before exhaustion sets in, adjust expectations before pressure escalates, or recognize and reduce intensity instead of adding more structure. A timely reset meets burnout while there's still room to respond—not after you've been pushed into stopping.

What a Timely Reset Actually Looks Like

A timely reset might mean stopping for the day instead of pushing through. It might mean postponing a decision until clarity returns, scaling back a commitment temporarily, or choosing one stabilizing action instead of many corrective ones.

The goal isn't perfection or productivity.
It's interruption.

Try This Now

Think about a recent moment when you noticed pressure rising.

Ask yourself:

- What signal did I feel first?
- How long did I wait before responding?
- What could a smaller, earlier reset look like next time for me?

You're not rewriting the past. You're practicing awareness for the future.

When Resetting Becomes a Skill

When you respond sooner, burnout doesn't escalate. Recovery takes less effort. Trust in yourself grows.

A reset stops feeling like a last resort.
It becomes a regular, supportive response—something you use to protect your energy and keep going.

That's how burnout loses its grip.

12

Life doesn't always slow down—**but you don't have to wait until you're out of step to adjust your pace.** *You can reset at any time and keep moving forward.*

Anytime Reset

A reset is often misunderstood.
It's commonly seen as something you do when things have gone wrong—when you've fallen behind, burned out, or lost control.

But a reset isn't a breakdown response.
It's a deliberate one.

A reset is the moment you notice something feels off and choose awareness over force—before pressure has a chance to take over. It's how you restore balance and stability before pressure turns into burnout.

A Reset is a Sign of Awareness

A reset doesn't mean you can't handle what's in front of you. It means you're noticing early enough to choose a different approach.

Capable people reset not because they've failed—but because they understand the cost of pushing past their limits for too long. Choosing a reset is choosing sustainability over strain, clarity over control, and long-term progress over short-term pressure.

Why a Reset Works When Willpower Doesn't

Burnout doesn't resolve itself through sheer determination. It resolves when pressure is adjusted, capacity is respected, and pace becomes intentional.

A reset works because it interrupts patterns before they escalate. It reduces strain instead of adding structure. It restores clarity before forcing action.

A reset doesn't demand more from you.
It supports you where you are.

A Reset Can Happen Anytime

A reset isn't a one-time event reserved for crisis moments. It can happen in the middle of a demanding season, halfway through a difficult day, or at the first sign that something feels off.

You don't have to wait for exhaustion to take over or for things to fall apart. Small, timely resets are often enough to change direction before burnout gains momentum.

What Changes Going Forward

What you've built through this book is awareness.

You now recognize early signals, understand capacity limits, and see the cost of pushing past them. That awareness shortens the distance between noticing and responding.

Each reset becomes easier.
Each recovery takes less time.
And trust in yourself continues to grow.

Try This Now

The next time you notice pressure rising, pause and ask yourself:

- Do I need to push through—or do I need a reset?
- What would a small, timely reset look like right now?

Then choose the option that supports you—not the one that proves something.

Resets are How You Keep Going

Resets don't slow your progress.
They preserve it.

They allow you to move forward without burning yourself out over and over again.

You adjust as life shifts, respond as capacity changes, and continue forward with intention.

That's the power of a reset, **anytime.**

Before You Go

If you've made it this far, I want to say something plainly.

Burnout doesn't mean you're incapable. It doesn't mean you've lost your edge. And it certainly doesn't mean you don't care enough.

In my experience — both personally and professionally — burnout shows up most often in capable people. The ones who show up. The ones who handle things. The ones who don't easily drop the ball.

That's why it can be so disorienting when something starts to feel off.

You don't collapse. You don't quit. You just feel different — heavier, less clear, less steady than you're used to.

This book wasn't written to fix you. It was written to give you language for what's happening — and a way to respond before depletion takes over.

You've seen that burnout builds quietly. That capacity shifts. That pace matters. That small adjustments can prevent bigger consequences.

More importantly, you've seen that resetting isn't dramatic. It's intentional. Timely. Often subtle.

It's choosing to pause when you're pushing too hard. Choosing to ease up when you're maxing out your intensity. Choosing to adjust your pace instead of forcing progress.

And here's the part I hope stays with you:

You don't have to wait until everything falls apart to adjust.

You don't have to earn the right to slow down.

You don't have to prove you can handle more.

You can reset when something feels off. You can reset before momentum turns into pressure. You can reset because you understand the cost of not doing so.

That's what changes the pattern. That's how burnout loses its grip. And that's something you can use — anytime.

Burnout Pattern Self-Assessment

Burnout rarely feels sudden when you look back at it.

It feels gradual. Layered. Predictable in hindsight.

This short reflection is designed to help you notice where burnout tends to build for you — not in theory, but in your real life.

There's no scoring.
No diagnosis.
No label.

Just awareness — so you can use a reset sooner next time.

Part 1: How Burnout Usually Begins for You

Think about the last time you felt burned out.

Answer honestly.

- What was increasing at the time — workload, emotional pressure, expectations, or something else?

- Were you adding responsibilities without removing any?
- Did you tell yourself it was temporary?
- Were you skipping breaks or rest because "now isn't the time"?

Write down what stands out.

Burnout patterns repeat because they feel familiar while you're in them.

Part 2: Your Early Signals

Before exhaustion forces a reset, signals usually show up.

For you, they might look like:

- Increased irritability
- Quiet anxiety
- Avoidance or procrastination
- Fear of making a new commitment
- Mental fog
- Loss of motivation

Add your own signals here:

What shifts first when your capacity is being exceeded?

The goal isn't to fix anything yet.
It's simply to recognize the earliest shift.

Part 3: Your Default Response

When pressure builds, most people default to one of two responses:

They push harder.
Or they shut down.

Which one feels more like you?

When strain increases, do you:

- Add more structure?
- Add more hours?
- Withdraw?
- Overcommit?
- Reorganize everything at once?

Your default response is often what keeps the burnout cycle moving.

Not because you're doing something wrong — but because it's automatic.

Part 4: Where the Pattern Breaks

Think about a time you avoided full burnout.

What did you do differently?

- Did you pause sooner?
- Lower expectations temporarily?
- Ask for help?

- Reduce intensity?
- Shift priorities?

Those moments matter.

They show you what works.

Closing Reflection

Burnout doesn't appear out of nowhere.

It builds along familiar lines.

The more clearly you see your pattern, the earlier you can use a reset.

And when a reset becomes something you do intentionally — not reactively — burnout loses much of its power.

B

The Anytime Reset Pattern

A simple framework you can internalize and reuse.

You don't need to reread this entire book every time something feels off.

You just need to remember the pattern.

Burnout builds in a pattern.
A reset follows one.

When you understand the pattern, you don't panic.
You move through it.

Here's the Anytime Reset pattern in its simplest form:

1. Notice the Drift

Burnout rarely arrives all at once.

It begins with small shifts:

- Increased tension
- Quiet anxiety
- Procrastination
- Fear of committing to something new

- Pushing just a little harder than usual

This is where most people miss it.

Not because they don't care — but because they're still functioning.

The first step is simply this:

Notice the drift.

Not dramatically.
Not critically.
Just honestly.

Something feels off.

That awareness alone shortens the distance to a reset.

2. Pause the Push

Once you notice the drift, your instinct may be to push harder.

Catch up.
Compensate.
Fix it quickly.

This is where burnout deepens.

Instead, pause.

Pause when you feel yourself pushing too hard.
Pause before effort turns into strain.

A pause doesn't mean stopping everything.

It means interrupting the automatic push long enough to regain perspective.

No overhaul.
No new system.
Just space.

3. Reduce the Load

After the pause, don't rebuild momentum by doing more.

Reduce.

Lower expectations temporarily.
Remove one unnecessary demand.
Scale back intensity instead of increasing structure.

You're not quitting.

You're adjusting effort to match capacity.

Reducing the load prevents recovery from turning into another burnout cycle.

4. Restore Stability

Before you accelerate again, stabilize.

Stability looks like:

- Less mental resistance
- Clearer thinking
- Fewer anxiety spikes
- The ability to stop without guilt

When stability returns, confidence returns with it.

Not because you forced it — but because you honored your limits.

Stability must come before speed if progress is going to last.

5. Resume at a Sustainable Pace

Now you move forward.

Not dramatically.
Not urgently.
Not to prove anything.

You move at a pace you can maintain.

That's the difference.

When you resume at a sustainable pace, burnout doesn't rebuild quietly underneath you.

You stay aware.
You adjust sooner.
You use a reset before pressure compounds.

Internalizing the Pattern

You don't need to memorize this word for word.

Just remember the rhythm:

Notice.
Pause.
Reduce.
Stabilize.
Resume.

Over time, this becomes automatic.

You'll feel the drift sooner.
You'll pause earlier.
You'll reduce intensity without guilt.
You'll restore stability before pushing again.

That's when a reset becomes a skill — not a reaction.

And that's when burnout stops running the pattern.

You do.

C

The 10-Minute Reset

A simple way to interrupt burnout before it escalates.

You don't always need an afternoon off.
You don't always need a new plan.

Sometimes you just need ten intentional minutes.

This short reset is designed for moments when:

- pressure is rising
- anxiety is building
- you're pushing harder than you should
- something feels off but you're still functioning

It's not dramatic.

It's preventative.

Minute 1–2: Stop the Push

Close your laptop.
Step away from the task.
Silence notifications if you can.

Take one slow breath.

You are not quitting.
You are interrupting.

Say it clearly to yourself:

"I'm pausing before this turns into strain."

That shift matters.

Minute 3–4: Check Your Capacity

Ask yourself:

- What is my energy level right now?
- Am I mentally clear or overloaded?
- What feels heavier than it should?

Don't judge the answers.

Just name them.

Capacity isn't a verdict.
It's information.

Minute 5–6: Reduce the Load

Choose one thing to soften.

- Delay one decision.
- Remove one unnecessary task.
- Lower one expectation.

- Send one message that buys you breathing room.

You don't need to fix everything.

You just need to reduce intensity.

Small reductions prevent large collapses.

Minute 7–8: Re-Establish Stability

Do something steadying.

Not productive.
Not corrective.
Steadying.

- Take a short walk.
- Drink water.
- Step outside.
- Sit quietly without input.
- Let your nervous system settle.

Stability first.
Speed later.

Minute 9–10: Choose Your Next Step

Now ask:

- What is the smallest, most reasonable next step?
- What can I complete without pushing?

Do that — and only that.

Not to prove anything.
Not to catch up.

Just to re-establish forward motion at a sustainable pace.

Why This Works

Burnout builds when pressure compounds without interruption.

A 10-minute reset interrupts the pattern.

It shortens the distance between signal and response. And when you respond sooner, recovery requires less effort.

You don't have to wait until you're exhausted.
You don't have to wait until everything feels overwhelming.

You can interrupt the pattern while you're still functioning. While you're still steady enough to choose differently.

That's the difference between recovery and prevention. Ten intentional minutes may not feel significant.

But prevention rarely feels dramatic.

It feels subtle.
Measured.
Quietly corrective.

When you respond early, strain doesn't have time to compound. Pressure doesn't have time to escalate.

And over time, those small interruptions change the pattern entirely.

A reset doesn't have to be long to be effective.
It just has to be timely.

That's what makes it sustainable.

D

Reset Energy Types

Why the way you reset matters.

Not everyone burns out the same way.

And not everyone resets the same way either.

Some people need structure.
Some need space.
Some need clarity.
Some need momentum.

If you've ever tried someone else's method and thought,
"Why doesn't this work for me?"
This is why.

A reset works best when it aligns with how you're wired.

Below is a light introduction to the Reset Energy Types used in the *Reset…Then Rise Again workshop.*

You don't need to diagnose yourself.
Just notice what resonates.

The Light Reclaimer

You reset by creating space.

When burnout builds, your system needs:

- quiet
- fewer inputs
- mental room to breathe

Too much structure feels suffocating.
Too many conversations feel draining.

A reset for you often looks like:

- stepping away
- reducing noise
- protecting your energy

Your power move: *Create space before you create plans.*

The Quiet Builder

You reset through small, steady progress.

When things feel off, you don't need a dramatic shift.
You need:

- manageable steps
- something you can complete
- proof you're still capable

Overhauls overwhelm you.
Tiny wins restore you.

Your power move: Finish something small before expanding.

The Momentum Maker

You reset by regaining forward motion.

When burnout hits, stagnation feels worse than effort.

But pushing too hard is what created the strain.

Your reset works best when you:

- stabilize first
- then move deliberately
- at a pace you can sustain

Your power move: Build stability before accelerating.

The Inner Fire Starter

You reset by reconnecting to meaning.

Burnout for you often feels like:

- losing enthusiasm

- losing direction
- losing connection to why something matters

Structure alone won't fix that.

You need:

- reflection
- clarity
- renewed purpose

Your power move: Reconnect before recommitting.

The Purpose Walker

You reset by aligning action with values.

Burnout builds when you feel:

- overextended
- misaligned
- pulled in too many directions

A reset for you often involves:

- reallocation
- recalibration
- simplifying commitments

Your power move: Adjust your path before adding pressure.

Why This Matters

There is no single right way to reset.

What restores one person can overwhelm another.

When you understand your energy tendencies, you stop forcing solutions that don't fit.

And a reset becomes easier — because it feels natural.

If you'd like a deeper exploration of your Energy Type — including personalized strategies and exercises — the *Reset… Then Rise Again workshop* walks you through that process step by step.

For now, just notice what resonates.

Awareness is the beginning of alignment.

Afterword

Resets are not something you graduate from. They're something you return to—whenever life shifts, pressure builds, or capacity changes.

If this book helped you recognize patterns sooner, slow down without guilt, or respond more intentionally, then it has done what it was meant to do.

At the same time, awareness is sometimes just the beginning. There are moments when you want more structure.
More guidance.
More space to think things through—without rushing or pushing yourself again.

This book was designed to help you recognize and interrupt burnout. The workshop exists to help you practice that interruption more deeply.

Reset…Then Rise Again is a self-paced online workshop designed to help you actively work through a reset. It builds on the same principles you've just read about, while offering more structure to help you recognize the onset of burnout, understand your energy patterns, and identify the approaches that work best for you personally.

The workshop allows you to:

- step back more intentionally
- examine where burnout shows up in your life
- reset your pace across multiple areas
- rebuild clarity without pressure

The six modules can be completed in as little as 2–3-hours, or at your own pace, whenever you're ready.

There's no urgency to move on to it.
You don't need to "fix" anything first.
When and if you want more structure, it's there to support you—not push you.

For now, remember this:

A reset isn't a setback.
It's a skill.
And it's one you can use anytime.

About the Author

Lorrie Penn Hunter is an entrepreneur, strategist, and longtime small business owner focused on creating practical, easy-to-implement solutions for entrepreneurs and self-employed professionals.

With more than 17 years in international business, marketing, and e-commerce, and 24+ years in real estate in the Washington Metro area, she has spent her career helping individuals and businesses navigate growth, change, and complexity. Her work also includes brand photography and small business strategy and marketing.

Through lived experience—and years of working alongside driven professionals—she has seen how consistent, persistent hustle can quietly lead to burnout, especially for those carrying multiple responsibilities. *Anytime Reset* was created to offer a resource she wished had been available earlier: one that is practical, grounded, and supportive without being overwhelming.

Lorrie is also active in public service and community organizations and brings nearly four decades of leadership, service, and mentorship into her work.

www.ingramcontent.com/pod-product-compliance
Lightning Source LLC
LaVergne TN
LVHW050936080826
845145LV00004B/1284

* 9 7 8 1 7 3 5 9 7 3 4 6 3 *